if...

A Mind-Bending New Way of Looking at Big Ideas and Numbers

Written by David J. Smith • Illustrated by Steve Adams

Kids Can Press

The big numbers and data in this book are factual, as far as we know. But nobody knows exactly how old Earth is, or exactly how big the Universe is, or exactly how big Earth's population is, or when the first animals appeared, or how many species there are. With really big numbers, there is lots of room for error. The data in this book is based on the most reliable estimates.

For teachers and colleagues who helped me to understand and appreciate our place in the Universe: Kathleen Raoul, Stan Sheldon, Mary Eliot, Ned Ryerson, Frederick S. Allis, Jack Schliemann, Bill Bellows, Anne McCormack, Jen Tobin, Jane Hardy and many others. And for the indomitable and endlessly supportive Val Wyatt. And always for Suzanne, my compass and my North Star. — D. J. S.

★

To Kaliane, Nick, Samantha, Stella-Rose and Victoria: Your little hands of today will do great things tomorrow! — S. A.

Text © 2014 David J. Smith
Illustrations © 2014 Steve Adams

Kids Can Press acknowledges the financial support of the Government of Ontario, through the Ontario Media Development Corporation's Ontario Book Initiative; the Ontario Arts Council; the Canada Council for the Arts; and the Government of Canada, through the CBF, for our publishing activity.

Published in Canada by
Kids Can Press Ltd.
25 Dockside Drive
Toronto, ON M5A 0B5

Published in the U.S. by
Kids Can Press Ltd.
2250 Military Road
Tonawanda, NY 14150

www.kidscanpress.com

Edited by Valerie Wyatt
Designed by Marie Bartholomew

This book is smyth sewn casebound.
Manufactured in Malaysia in 3/2014 by Tien Wah Press (Pte) Ltd.

CM 14 0 9 8 7 6 5 4 3 2 1

LIBRARY AND ARCHIVES CANADA CATALOGUING IN PUBLICATION

Smith, David J. (David Julian), 1944 –, author
   If : a mind-bending new way of looking at big ideas and numbers / written by David J. Smith ; illustrated by Steve Adams.

ISBN 978-1-894786-34-8 (bound)

   1. Astronomy — Juvenile literature. 2. World history — Juvenile literature.
3. Population — Juvenile literature. 4. Natural resources — Juvenile literature.
5. Natural history — Juvenile literature.

I. Adams, Steve, illustrator II. Title.

Q163.S65 2014   j500   C2013-907498-8

Kids Can Press is a corus™ Entertainment company

Contents

If 4

Our Galaxy 6

The Planets 8

History of Earth 10

Life on Earth 12

Events of the Last 3000 Years 14

Inventions through Time 16

Inventions of the Last 1000 Years 18

The Continents 20

Water 22

Species of Living Things 24

Money 26

Energy 28

Life Expectancy 30

Population 32

Food 34

Your Life 36

A Note for Parents and Teachers 38

Sources 40

iF...

How big is Earth or the Solar System or the Milky Way galaxy?
How old is our planet and when did the first animals and people appear on it?
Some things are so huge or so old that it's hard to wrap your mind around them.
But what if we took these big, hard-to-imagine objects and events and compared
them to things we can see, feel and touch? Instantly, we'd see our world in a
whole new way. That's what this book is about — it scales down, or shrinks,
huge events, spaces and times to something we can understand.
If you've had a doll or a model airplane, you know what scaling down means.
A scale model is a small version of a large thing. Every part is reduced
equally, so that you don't end up with a doll with enormous feet
or a model plane with giant wings.
And when we scale down some really huge things — such as the
Solar System or all of human history — some of the results are
quite surprising, as you are about to see ...

OUR GALAXY

iF the Milky Way galaxy were shrunk to the size of a dinner plate ...

* our whole Solar System — the Sun and the planets — would be far smaller than this speck of dust, too small to see

* the visible Universe, on the other hand, would be about the size of Belgium.

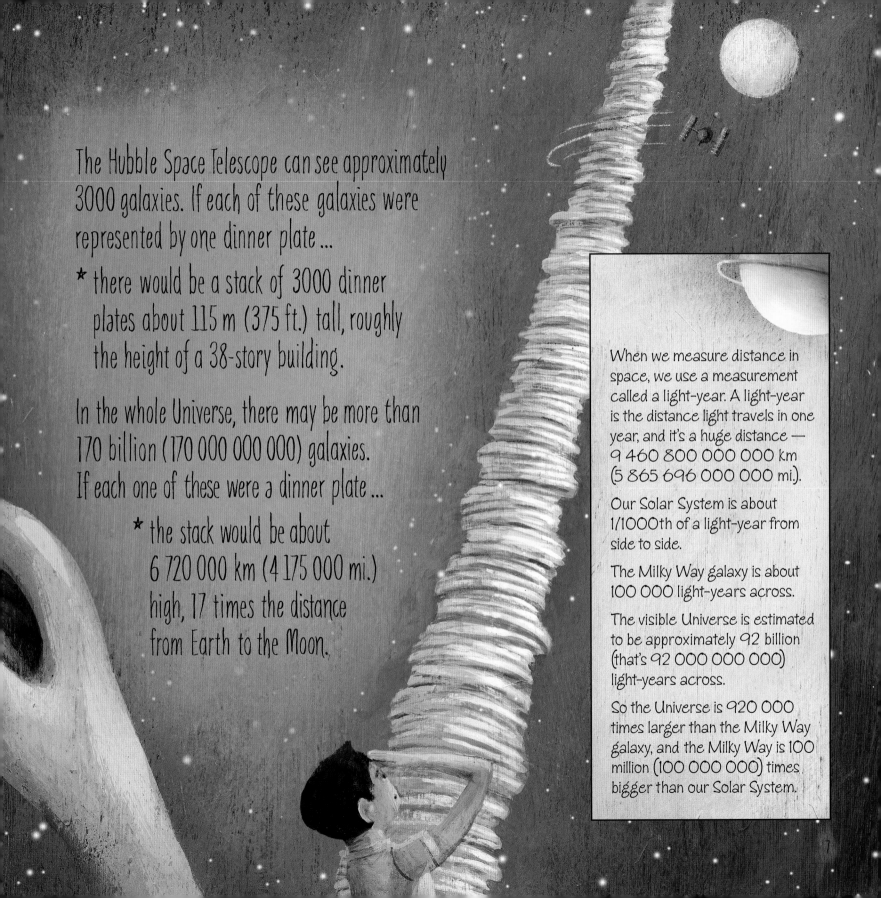

The Hubble Space Telescope can see approximately 3000 galaxies. If each of these galaxies were represented by one dinner plate ...

* there would be a stack of 3000 dinner plates about 115 m (375 ft.) tall, roughly the height of a 38-story building.

In the whole Universe, there may be more than 170 billion (170 000 000 000) galaxies. If each one of these were a dinner plate ...

* the stack would be about 6 720 000 km (4 175 000 mi.) high, 17 times the distance from Earth to the Moon.

When we measure distance in space, we use a measurement called a light-year. A light-year is the distance light travels in one year, and it's a huge distance — 9 460 800 000 000 km (5 865 696 000 000 mi.).

Our Solar System is about 1/1000th of a light-year from side to side.

The Milky Way galaxy is about 100 000 light-years across.

The visible Universe is estimated to be approximately 92 billion (that's 92 000 000 000) light-years across.

So the Universe is 920 000 times larger than the Milky Way galaxy, and the Milky Way is 100 million (100 000 000) times bigger than our Solar System.

THE PLANETS

IF the planets in the Solar System were shrunk to the size of balls and Earth were the size of a baseball ...

* Mercury would be about the size of a Ping-Pong ball
* Venus, a tennis ball
* Mars, a golf ball
* Jupiter, an exercise ball
* Saturn, a beach ball
* Uranus, a basketball
* Neptune, a soccer ball.

The Sun would be bigger than any ball, about 10 times the diameter of Jupiter.

8

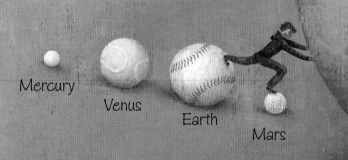

Mercury

Venus

Earth

Mars

Jupiter

IF the planets in the Solar System were laid out on a 100-yard football field, and the Sun were the size of a grapefruit on one goal line ...

* Mercury would be on the 4-yard line, Venus on the 7, Earth on the 10 and Mars on the 15. Each would be about the size of a grain of salt.

* Jupiter would be a large pea just beyond the midfield line and Saturn a smaller pea on the opposite goal line.

* Uranus and Neptune, each the size of a sesame seed, would be out of sight, far beyond the goal line.

Saturn

Uranus

Neptune

HISTORY OF EARTH

iF the 4.5-billion-year history of Earth were compressed into a single year...

January
February
March
April
May
June
July
August
September
October

iF the entire history of Earth from its very beginning were a two-hour DVD, humans would appear in the last second of the video.

* on January 1, Earth forms

* around the middle of February, the Moon appears. In the third week of February, the oceans and atmosphere appear, as does the landmass that will eventually break up and become the continents.

* by the third week of March, the first life-forms appear in the sea

* in April, more complex life-forms appear in the sea

* toward the middle of June, oxygen is released into the atmosphere from algae and other microscopic life in the sea, paving the way for living things that breathe oxygen. In late June, the first great ice age occurs.

* in early November, another great ice age occurs and more complex life-forms, such as small fish, arrive. From the end of November to the middle of December, many new kinds of life evolve, and the first animals appear on land.

* around December 18, the first birds emerge. Close to December 22, mammals evolve. Near the last day of December, humans appear.

11

LIFE ON EARTH

If the 3.5 billion years of life on Earth were reduced to one hour ...

* the first life-forms — one-celled organisms such as bacteria — appear in the first second of the hour

* fish show up at 51 minutes and 10 seconds, and amphibians appear at 54 minutes, 10 seconds

* the dinosaurs arrive at 56 minutes and are gone 3 minutes later

* mammals appear at 56 minutes, 25 seconds

* the earliest birds appear at 58 minutes

* our earliest human ancestors finally make an appearance at 59 minutes, 56 seconds

* modern humans—the humans we are related to—show up at 59 minutes, 59.8 seconds.

iF the time frame were one day — 24 hours instead of 1 hour — then the first life-forms appear just after midnight, fish at 8:28 p.m., the first mammals at 10:36 p.m. and our earliest human ancestors at about 24 minutes before midnight. Modern humans show up at 5 seconds before midnight, just as the day is ending.

EVENTS OF THE LAST 3000

Sunday	Monday	Tuesday	Wednesday
	1 Use of iron becomes widespread.	**2**	**3** First Olympic Games are held (776 BCE).
7 Alexander the Great builds a vast empire (336–323 BCE).	**8** Great Wall of China is built (221 BCE).	**9**	**10** Jesus Christ is born (5 BCE).
14	**15** The Middle Ages begin.	**16** Muhammad is born (570).	**17**
21 William the Conqueror invades England and becomes king (1066).	**22**	**23** Genghis Khan becomes head of the Mongols (1206).	**24** The Black Death ravages Europe (1347–1350).
28 The French Revolution begins (1789) and ends (1799).	**29** Alexander Graham Bell invents the telephone (1876).	**30** The first computer is built (1939). The Internet is created (1969).	**31** Evidence of water is discovered on Mars (2013).

YEARS

IF the history of the last 3000 years were condensed into one month ...

Thursday	Friday	Saturday
4	**5** Buddha is born (560 BCE). Confucius is born (551 BCE).	**6**
11 City of Pompeii is destroyed by Vesuvius eruption (79 CE).	**12** Paper is invented in China (105 CE).	**13**
18 Medicine and the sciences flourish in Arab Spain (around 750).	**19**	**20** Vikings are the first Europeans to reach North America (late 900s).
25 Columbus reaches the Americas (1492).	**26** African slaves are first shipped to the Americas (1510).	**27** The dodo bird goes extinct (1690).

15

INVENTIONS THROUGH TIME

IF all the inventions and discoveries humans have made were laid out along a measuring tape 36 inches long ...

At one end is the first human discovery — fire. People first used fire about 790 000 years ago to keep themselves warm and to cook their food.

About halfway along, humans first build shelters.

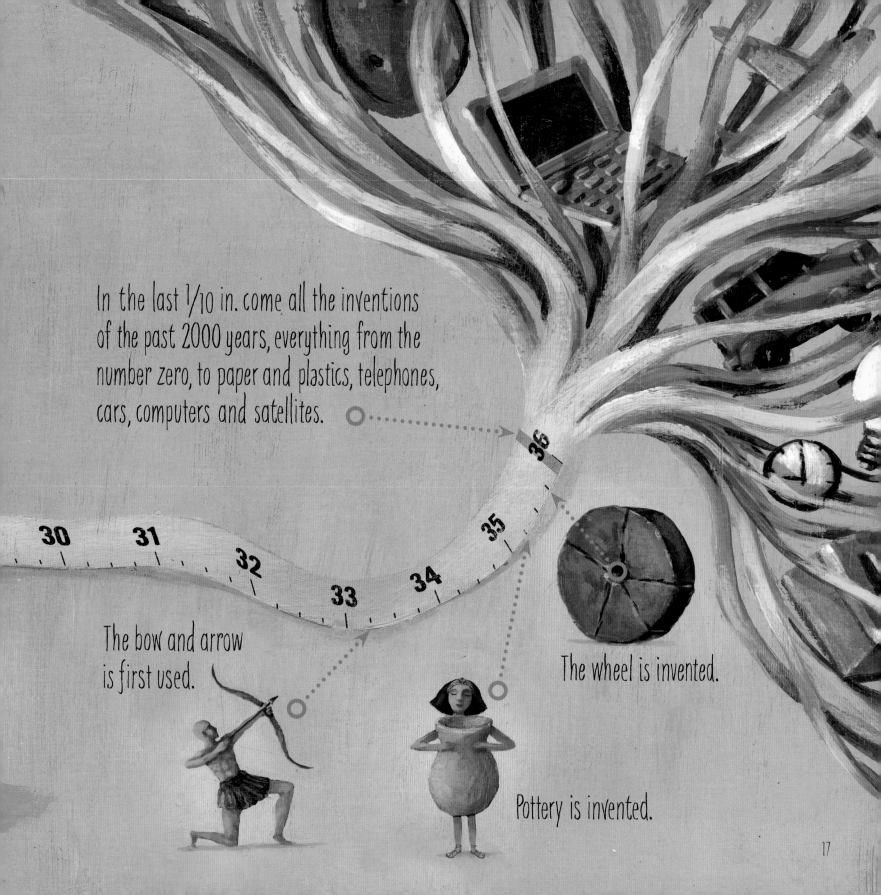

In the last 1/10 in. come all the inventions of the past 2000 years, everything from the number zero, to paper and plastics, telephones, cars, computers and satellites.

30 31 32 33 34 35 36

The bow and arrow is first used.

The wheel is invented.

Pottery is invented.

17

INVENTIONS OF THE LAST

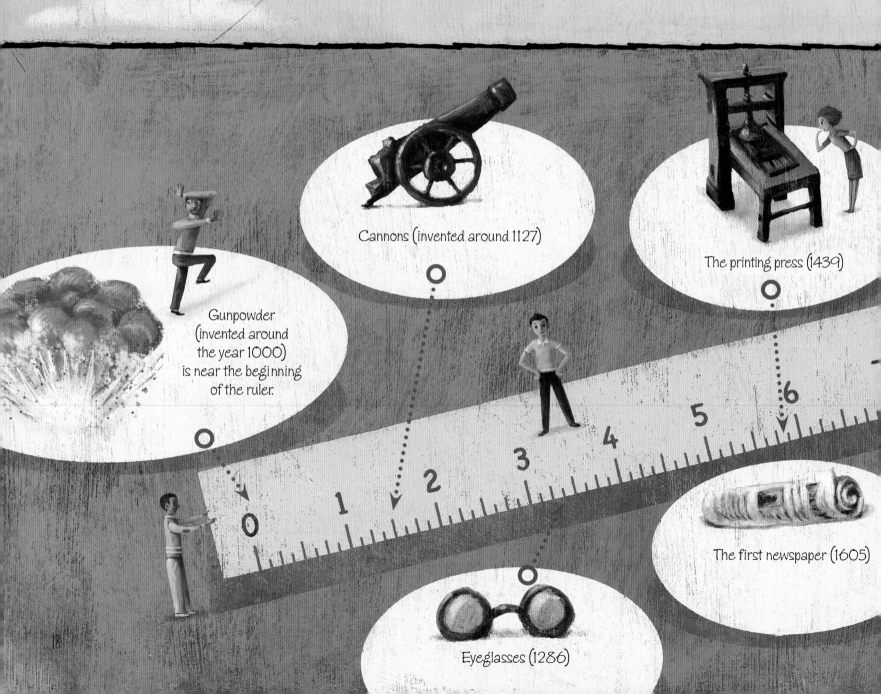

Cannons (invented around 1127)

The printing press (1439)

Gunpowder (invented around the year 1000) is near the beginning of the ruler.

The first newspaper (1605)

Eyeglasses (1286)

1000 YEARS

iF the inventions of the last 1000 years were laid out along this ruler...

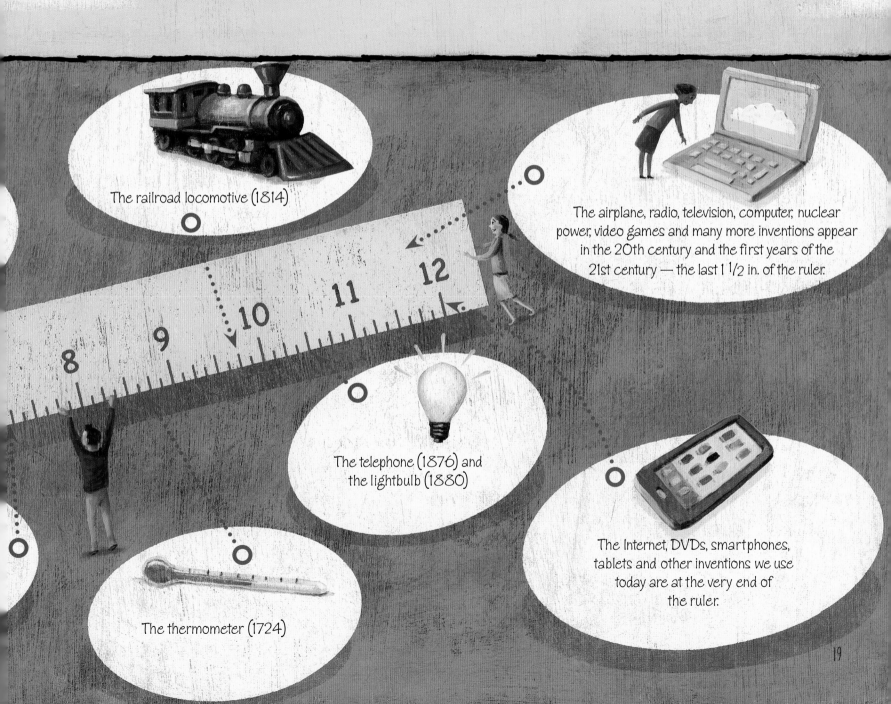

The railroad locomotive (1814)

The airplane, radio, television, computer, nuclear power, video games and many more inventions appear in the 20th century and the first years of the 21st century — the last 1 1/2 in. of the ruler.

The telephone (1876) and the lightbulb (1880)

The Internet, DVDs, smartphones, tablets and other inventions we use today are at the very end of the ruler.

The thermometer (1724)

19

THE CONTINENTS

IF the surface of Earth were shrunk to fit two pages of this book...

* three-quarters would be in blue for the seas and oceans
* the remaining one-quarter would be in different colors for the continents:

    - Asia would take up about 7.5% of Earth's surface

    - Africa 5%

    - North America 4.1%

    - South America 3%

    - Antarctica 2.3%

    - Europe 1.7%

    - Oceania (Australia, New Zealand and the other islands of the Pacific) 1.4%.

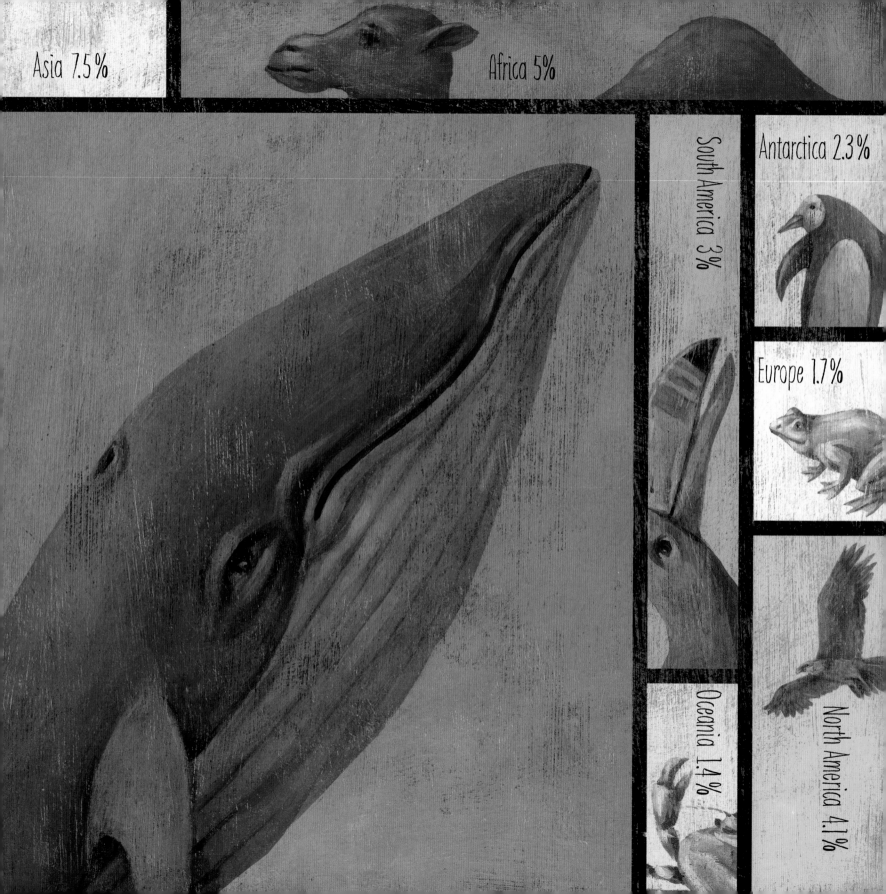

Asia 7.5%

Africa 5%

South America 3%

Antarctica 2.3%

Europe 1.7%

Oceania 1.4%

North America 4.1%

WATER

iF all the water
on Earth were
represented
by 100 glasses ...

* 97 of the glasses would
  be filled with salt water
  from the oceans and some lakes

* 3 of the glasses would contain fresh
  water. One of these glasses would represent
  all the fresh water available to us. The rest of the
  fresh water is locked up in glaciers, frozen in
  the atmosphere or inaccessible deep underground.

22

Who uses the water and for what? We use about 10% of all the Earth's water in and around our homes — for drinking, cooking, washing and other household needs. People in America use about 2 1/2 bathtubs of water per person a day for household purposes. In Europe, it's about 2 bathtubs full. In Africa, that number falls as low as 1/10 of a bathtub, even though the United Nations says that 1/4 bathtub of water per person is needed for health and well-being.

Household needs are small compared with water used in industry and agriculture. Industry uses twice as much water as households do — about 20% of all the world's water. And agriculture uses 70% of Earth's water. So the places that use the most water are the places that have the most water-intensive agriculture. Asia, in particular, is responsible for about 3/4 of the water use in the world.

SPECIES OF LIVING THINGS

IF all species of living things on Earth were represented by a tree with 1000 leaves ...

* 753 leaves would be animals —
including every multi-celled animal,
from beetles to cats to humans to whales

 **TIC TOC** How fast are species disappearing? Long ago, about one leaf disappeared from the tree every 1000 years. (One leaf represents 1750 known species.) However, today extinctions are happening at a faster rate, mainly because of habitat destruction and loss. As a result, some scientists predict that our tree with its 1000 leaves may lose as many as 200 leaves in the next 20 years or so. But new species are being discovered all the time, so new leaves are also being added to the tree.

* about 46 leaves would be protozoa — one-celled,
animal-like organisms — and algae together

* 41 leaves would be fungi, such
as mushrooms and yeast

* 154 leaves would be plants

* 6 leaves would
be bacteria

MONEY

If all the wealth in the world — about 223 trillion (223 000 000 000 000) U.S. dollars — were represented by a pile of 100 coins ...

* the richest 1% of the world's population would have 40 of the coins
* 9 % would have 45 coins
* 40 % would have 14 coins
* the poorest 50 % — half the world's population — would share just one coin.

If the 100 coins were divided among the continents, here's where they would be ...

North America, 32 coins

Europe, 34 coins

Asia, 22 coins

Africa, 3 coins

South America, 6 coins

Oceania, 3 coins

ENERGY

iF all the energy sources in the world were represented by 100 lightbulbs...

* 2 lightbulbs would be powered by hydroelectric power
* 6 by nuclear energy
* 11 by renewable energy — wind, geothermal and biomass
* 21 by gas
* 27 by coal
* 33 by oil.

In other words, fossil fuels (gas, coal and oil) would power 81 of the 100 lightbulbs.

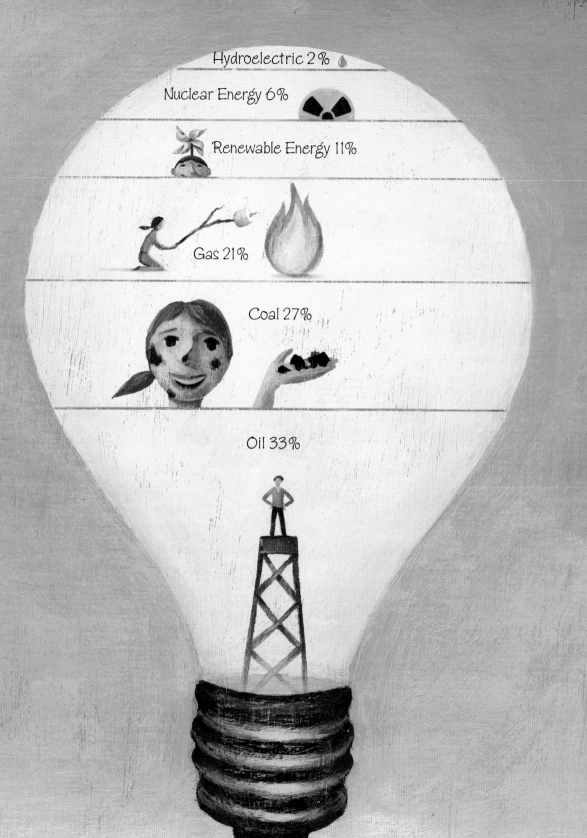

Hydroelectric 2%

Nuclear Energy 6%

Renewable Energy 11%

Gas 21%

Coal 27%

Oil 33%

iF all the world's energy consumption were a big chocolate bar with 12 squares ...

* people in Asia and Oceania (Australia, New Zealand and the other islands of the Pacific) would consume 4 squares

* Europeans, 3

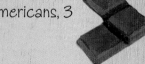

* North Americans, 3

* Africans, 1

* people in Central and South America, 1.

LIFE EXPECTANCY

iF average life expectancy (the number of years people live) were represented by footprints in the sand...

* the average person would leave 70 steps, because average life expectancy is 70 years. But that's an average. Not everyone leaves 70 steps.

* South Americans, 74

* Asians, 70 steps

* Africans would leave 58 steps

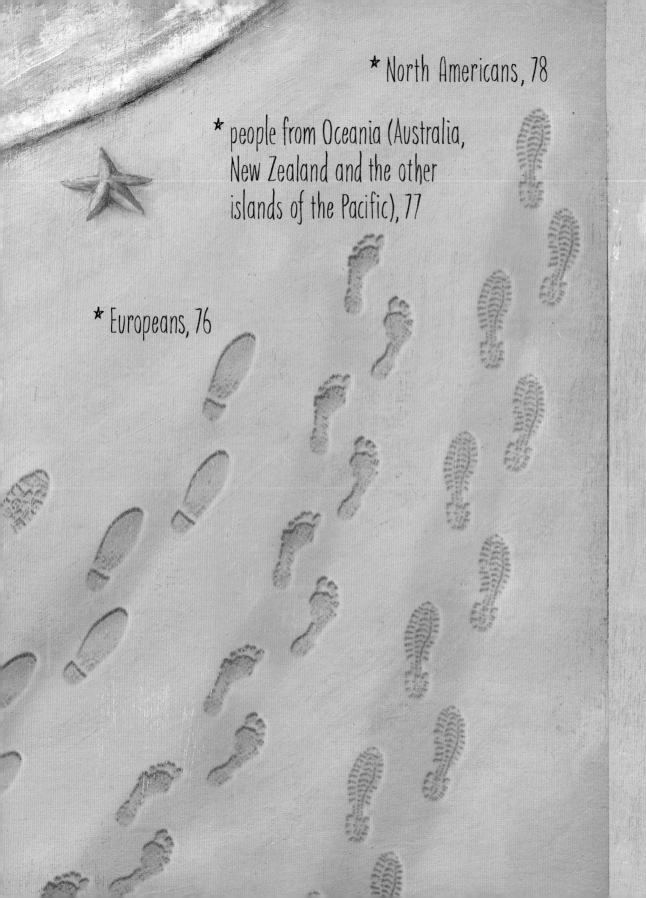

* North Americans, 78

* people from Oceania (Australia, New Zealand and the other islands of the Pacific), 77

* Europeans, 76

The people with the longest trail of footprints (highest life expectancy) are from these countries:

*Japan, Switzerland and San Marino (83 steps each)

*Andorra, Australia, Canada, France, Iceland, Israel, Italy, Luxembourg, Monaco, Qatar, Singapore, Spain and Sweden (82).

People with the lowest life expectancy are from these countries:

* Guinea-Bissau, Lesotho, Somalia and Swaziland (50 steps each)

* Democratic Republic of the Congo (49)

* Central African Republic (48)

* Sierra Leone (47).

31

POPULATION

IF today's world population of over 7 billion were represented by a village of 100 people ...

* in 1900, there would have been only 32 people in the village because the world's population was much smaller

* in 1800, 17 people

* in 1000 BCE, only 1 person would have lived in the village

* in 1650, 10 people

* in 1500, 8 people

* in 1 CE, 3 people

Around the world, 15 000 babies are born every hour, and 6432 people die. That means in the 10 or so seconds it takes you to read this sentence, 42 babies have been born, and 17 people have died, increasing Earth's population by 25.

If the world's population keeps growing at its current rate, there will be 129 people in the village by 2050 instead of 100.

FOOD

IF all the food produced around the world in one year were represented by a loaf of bread with 25 slices ...

* 11 slices of bread would come from Asia
* 5 from South and Central America
* 4 from Europe
* 2 ¾ from North America
* 2 from Africa
* ¼ from Oceania.

IF all the food *consumed* around the world in one year were represented by a loaf of bread with 25 slices ...

· 13 ½ slices would be eaten by Asians
· 4 ¼ by Europeans
· 2 ¾ by South and Central Americans
· 2 ½ by Africans
· 1 ¾ by North Americans
· ¼ by people from Oceania (Australia, New Zealand and other islands of the Pacific).

YOUR LIFE

iF your whole life could be shown as a jumbo pizza, divided into 12 slices ...

4 slices would be the time you spend in school or at work

1 slice would be spent shopping, caring for others and doing things around home

1 slice would be spent traveling — to school, work and shops — and on holidays

4 slices would be the time you spend getting ready to sleep and sleeping

1 slice would be the time you spend preparing food and eating

the last slice would be spent on leisure and recreation, such as exercise, games, social activities and surfing the Internet

A Note for Parents and Teachers

Our world and our Universe are full of things that are just too big to grasp. By scaling them down, we can bring them into focus.

Scale is a useful tool for architects, engineers, medical researchers and model builders. But it's also an important part of numeracy — understanding what numbers mean and how to use them. Our children need to be numerate so that they can become informed citizens when they grow up.

My interest in scale began when I was a young boy, building model ships. As a teacher, I used a lot of activities related to models and scale to get children thinking about the sizes and relationships of big things. These exercises taught me just how powerful scales and modeling can be. From ideas like this came my books *If the World Were a Village*, *If America Were a Village* and *This Child, Every Child*. They scale down big ideas and issues into something more digestible, more meaningful.

Here are some activities to use with children to help them understand scale.

Start a scale collection

Children are surrounded by objects that have been scaled down, such as dolls, toy cars and dinosaurs. Gather some toys and help children figure out their scale. For example, a real *Tyrannosaurus rex* was about 12 m (40 ft.) long. Measure a scaled-down *T. rex* model and figure out its scale. Let's say the toy dinosaur is 10 cm (4 in.) long. A life-size *T. rex* at 12 m is 1200 cm, so the scale of this model *T. rex* would be 10:1200, which would be expressed as 1:120. In inches, the scale would be 4:480, or 1:120.

Maps

Maps are another common example of scale in our lives. They take something large (city, state, country, world) and scale it down to something you can hold in your hand and use. A map usually provides information about its scale, given as a proportion that represents the size of the map compared to the size of the original. A wall map of the United States or Canada may say 1:5 000 000 — 1 centimeter or inch on the map = 5 000 000 centimeters or inches in the world. Try mapping your school, home or neighborhood and see which scale works best for a map that's convenient to hold and use.

Earth apple

This inspiring Earth-shrinking activity was developed in 1994 by Population Connection. It has since appeared all around the world. A link can be found on the Sources page (page 40).

The activity compares Earth to an apple. Remove three-quarters of the apple. This represents Earth's water (oceans, ice, lakes and rivers). The remaining quarter is land. Cut the land quarter in half. One of these chunks represents land that is uninhabited, inhospitable to people and crops (the polar regions, deserts, swamps, high mountains and so on). The remaining piece, one-eighth of the Earth, is the area where people can comfortably live.

Now slice this little one-eighth segment into four pieces. Three of the pieces represent land that can't be farmed — the land is too rocky, wet, cold, steep or

has soil too thin for agriculture, or it is land that was once farmed but has been turned into cities, highways and other human developments. Set them aside. The last slice — one thirty-second of the Earth's surface — is the land we have for growing food. That tiny slice has to feed all the people on Earth.

Time lines

A time line is a great tool for the classroom, especially for social studies. Unroll a big roll of paper and tape it to the walls around your classroom in one long sheet. Mark one end with the date your social studies program begins (for example, 1492, 1776, etc.) and the other end with "Today." Then figure out how many inches or centimeters would represent the years between. As your studies progress, add events. For example, if your topic is colonial history, you might add: 1603, Champlain maps New France; 1609, Virginia Colony; 1620, Plymouth and so on.

A time line can be used for many topics — European history, the English monarchy, U.S. presidents, inventions, etc.

Time lines don't have to be horizontal. Ask children to imagine a vertical time line by visualizing a coin and a stamp balanced on top of the Eiffel Tower. If the entire height of the tower + coin + stamp represents the history of Earth, then coin + stamp shows the time humans have been on the planet, and the stamp is recorded history, about 3000 years. Discuss with children what other ways there might be to imagine time and its passage.

Matching scales

Draw outlines of animals in chalk on a large patch of pavement. (If no outdoor space is available, use a floor or even a large sheet of paper.) Start with a blue whale — Earth's largest animal. Since a life-size blue whale would be about 30 m (100 ft.) long, you'll need to scale it down to something more manageable. Nearby, draw other animals to match the scale of your blue whale.

Or compare the areas of countries. The biggest country is Russia, the smallest is Vatican City, and the others fall somewhere in between.

Scaling up

For another activity, try scaling up small things. Many towns celebrate something important to them with a large-scale version. For example, Alma, Arkansas, has the world's largest spinach can, while Moose Jaw, Saskatchewan, has a huge moose, and Tampa, Florida, has a gigantic bowling pin. What would be a good symbol for your family or school? Decide on something and help children work out the scale they would like it to be. Then help them calculate the dimensions of the scaled-up symbol.

Or scale up a small picture or map. Divide the picture you want to scale up into sections by making a grid. Make a larger grid on a blank piece of paper. Then copy each of the sections of the small picture onto the equivalent sections of the larger grid.

Most of all, have fun, explore possibilities and contact me through my website if you have an activity to share: http://www.mapping.com/if.

David J. Smith

Sources

Books for Children

A Cool Drink of Water, by Barbara Kerley. Washington: National Geographic Society, 2006.

If America Were a Village, by David J. Smith. Toronto: Kids Can Press, 2009.

If the World Were a Village, second edition, by David J. Smith. Toronto: Kids Can Press, 2011.

One Well: The Story of Water on Earth, by Rochelle Strauss. Toronto: Kids Can Press, 2007.

Tree of Life: The Incredible Biodiversity of Life on Earth, by Rochelle Strauss. Toronto: Kids Can Press, 2004.

Books and Reports

Goode's World Atlas, edited by J. Paul Goode and others. Skokie, IL: Rand McNally, 2003, 2009.

Hubble: A Journey Through Space and Time, by Edward Weiler. New York: Abrams, 2010.

Powers of Ten: About the Relative Size of Things in the Universe, by Philip Morrison, Phylis Morrison and the Office of Charles and Ray Eames. Based on the film *Powers of Ten* by Charles and Ray Eames. Santa Monica, CA: Eames Office, 1994.

The Planets, by Dava Sobel. New York: Viking Penguin, 2005.

State of the World, 2012: Moving Toward Sustainable Prosperity. State of the World, 2011: Innovations That Nourish the Planet. State of the World, 2010: Transforming Cultures from Consumerism to Sustainability. Washington: Worldwatch Institute.

The World Almanac and Book of Facts, edited by Sarah Janssen. New York: Infobase Publishing, 2010, 2011, 2012.

World Development Indicators. Washington: World Bank, 2010, 2011, 2012.

Websites

More than a hundred websites, including Wikipedia, were used during the course of researching this book. Some of the most useful were:

CIA World Factbook for world statistics and for comparing or referencing different countries: https://www.cia.gov/library/publications/the-world-factbook

EcoKids for biodiversity: http://www.ecokids.ca/pub/eco_info/topics/biodiversity/species.cfm

Food and Agriculture Organization of the United Nations for information on food and food consumption: http://www.fao.org; the FAO Hunger Portal http://www.fao.org/hunger/en/#jfmulticontent_c130584-2; FAO Statistics Gateway http://faostat3.fao.org/faostat-gateway/go/to/home/E

NASA for space: http://www.nasa.gov

Population Connection and its Population Education program for "Earth: The Apple of Our Eye": http://www.populationeducation.org

The Population Reference Bureau for current and historic population data: http://www.prb.org

U.S. Census Bureau International Programs for current and historic population data: https://www.census.gov/population/international/data/idb/informationGateway.php

U.S. Geological Survey (USGS) for water use: http://ga.water.usgs.gov/edu/earthhowmuch.html

World Bank for information on money and wealth: http://www.worldbank.org; World Bank Data Gateway http://data.worldbank.org

World Resources Simulation Centre for water, climate and food: http://www.wrsc.org

DISCARD